Tash Fairbanks a

Fo

Methuen Drama

Published by Methuen Drama 2012

Methuen Drama, an imprint of Bloomsbury Publishing Plc

1 3 5 7 9 10 8 6 4 2

Methuen Drama
Bloomsbury Publishing Plc
50 Bedford Square
London WC1B 3DP
www.methuendrama.com

First published by Methuen Drama in 2012

ISBN 978 1 408 17239 1

A CIP catalogue record for this book is available from the British Library

Available in the USA from Bloomsbury Academic & Professional, 175 Fifth
Avenue/3rd Floor, New York, NY 10010. www.BloomsburyAcademicUSA.com

Typeset by Mark Heslington Ltd, Scarborough, North Yorkshire
Printed and bound in Great Britain by CPI Group (UK) Ltd, Croydon CR0 4YY

New Writing at the Finborough Theatre Season
November 2011 to January 2012

AGF Productions in association with Neil McPherson for the
Finborough Theatre presents

The World Premiere

FOG

by Tash Fairbanks and Toby Wharton

FINBOROUGH | THEATRE

First performance at the Finborough Theatre: Tuesday, 3 January 2012.

FOG

by Tash Fairbanks and Toby Wharton

Cast in order of appearance

Gary ('Fog')	**Toby Wharton**
Cannon	**Victor Gardener**
Michael	**Benjamin Cawley**
Bernice	**Kanga Tanikye-Buah**
Lou	**Annie Hemingway**

Present day. Winter. Council tower block. Could be any estate in London.

The performance lasts approximately seventy-five minutes.

There will be no interval.

Director	**Ché Walker**
Designer	**Georgia Lowe**
Lighting Designer	**Arnim Friess**
Sound Designer	**Edward Lewis**
Costume Designer	**Rachel Szmukler**
Fight Director	**Steve Medlin**
Stage Manager	**Arezou Ali**

Kanga Tanikye-Buah | Bernice

Trained at Arts Educational Schools London.

Theatre includes *The Tempest* (Orange Tree Theatre, Richmond), *Sonnet Walk* (Shakespeare's Globe) and rehearsed readings of *Fog* (Lyric Theatre, Hammersmith) and *364* (The Lyric Lounge).

Film includes *English in Mind Level 4* and *English in Mind Level 5*.

Radio includes *Ethood* advert.

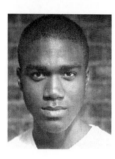

Benjamin Cawley | Michael

Theatre includes *Sense* (Hen and Chickens Theatre), *Sticks and Stones* (Old Red Lion Theatre), *Dunsinane* (Royal Shakespeare Company at the Hampstead Theatre), *Dark Carnival* (Old Vic Tunnels), *Crossing the Line, Patterns of Grace* (Hampstead Theatre), *Who Let the Dogs Out* (Soho Theatre), *O.O.L.P.O.S.P, There is Nothing There* (Oval House Theatre) and *Other Voices* (Rose Theatre, Kingston).

Television includes *How TV Ruined Your Life* and *Flash Prank*.

Radio includes *Switching Lanes*.

Victor Gardener | Cannon

Trained at Lee Strasberg Institute, New York, and Webber Douglas.

Theatre includes *Macbeth, Miss Julie, Of Mice and Men, The Caretaker, Blood Wedding, Arturo Ui, Road, A Midsummer Night's Dream, The Recruiting Officer, Europeans* (Mercury Theatre, Colchester), *Doorman* (Theatre Royal, Plymouth), *The Way of the World* (Wilton's Music Hall), *Bollywood Jane* (West Yorkshire Playhouse), *Macbeth* (Belfast Festival at Queen's), *Blocked* (Lyric Theatre, Belfast), *The Taming of the Shrew* (United States Tour), *Enjoy* (Theatre Royal Bath) and *Biblical Tales* (New End Theatre, Hampstead).

Television includes *Law and Order UK, Casualty, The Crux, Doctors, The Bill, Emmerdale* and *Murphy's Law*.

Film includes *Fortune's Smile, Postcode, The Fourth Dimension* and *Doctor Surreal*.

Annie Hemingway | Lou

Trained at the Royal Academy of Dramatic Art.

Theatre includes *Richard III* (Royal Shakespeare Company), *Baghdad Wedding* (Soho Theatre), *She Stoops to Conquer* (Birmingham Rep), *Chauntecleer and Pertelotte* (Old Red Lion Theatre and Brighton Fringe Festival), *Breakfast at Tiffany's* (Theatre Royal Haymarket), *Mrs Reynolds and the Ruffian* (Watford Palace Theatre), *Love's Labour's Lost* (Guildford Shakespeare Company), *T.S. Eliot Exchange Project* (Old Vic New Voices and Vineyard Theatre, New York) and *The Syndicate* (Chichester Festival Theatre).

Toby Wharton | Gary ('Fog') | Playwright

Trained at the Royal Academy of Dramatic Art.

Theatre includes *Shalom Baby* (Theatre Royal Stratford East), *Days of Significance* (Royal Shakespeare Company), *Ajax* (Riverside Studios), *Transient* (Pleasance Edinburgh and Shunt Vaults Theatre), *Home* (Tristan Bates Theatre) and *Six Days* (Camden People's Theatre).

Film and television includes *Postcode*, *Bashment*, *Silent Witness*, *The Bill* and *Gates*.

Fog is Toby's first play.

Tash Fairbanks | Playwright

Tash was born in 1948. A writer, theatrical performer and playwright, she trained at E15 Acting School and was a founder member of the lesbian feminist Siren Theatre Company in 1979. Her playwriting includes commissions for Theatre of Thelema, Women's Theatre Group, Graeae, Theatre Centre, Charter Theatre Company and Siren Theatre Company with such works as *Mama's Gone a Hunting* (1980), *Curfew* (1982), *From the Divine* (1983), *Now Wash Your Hands Please* (1984), *Pulp* (1985), *Hotel Destiny* (1987) and *Swamp* (1989) which have toured extensively in the UK, Holland, Germany and the USA. Film includes *Nocturne* (Channel 4). Her published work includes *Siren Plays* (Taylor & Francis) and *Fearful Symmetry* (Onlywomen Press). Her work as an actor includes productions for Sidewalk Theatre, Gay Sweatshop, Theatre of Thelema and Siren Theatre Company, as well as receiving a nomination from *Plays and Players* for Best New Actress of the Year.

Ché Walker | Director

Che returns to the Finborough Theatre where he made his directorial debut with *Achidi J's Final Hours* (2004) and has directed two other sell-out productions – *Etta Jenks*, starring Daniela Nardini and Clarke Peters (2005), and *Blue Surge* (2011).

Other theatre includes *Been So Long* (Young Vic and English Touring Theatre), *Extended Family* (Chichester Festival Theatre), *The Glory of Living* (BAC), *Estate Walls, Little Baby Jesus* (Oval House), *Lovesong* (English Touring Theatre and Edinburgh Fringe), *Car Thieves* (National Theatre Studio) and *Dance for Me* (Tricycle Theatre). Ché's writing includes *Been So Long* (Young Vic and Royal Court Theatre), *The Frontline* (Shakespeare's Globe), *Iphigenia* (Southwark Playhouse), *Flesh Wound* (Royal Court Theatre), *Crazy Love* (Paines Plough), *Car Thieves* (National Theatre Studio), *Carmen* (Open Air Theatre), *Dance For Me* (Theatre Royal Stratford East) and *Rootz Spectacular* (Belgrade Theatre, Coventry). He is also writing the book for *The Eighth*, a new musical with music and lyrics by Paul Heaton of The Beautiful South for this year's Manchester International Festival as well as writing his own musical adaptation of *The Bacchae* with Arthur Darvill for English Touring Theatre. This year, Ché will direct the feature film adaptation of his original musical *Been So Long* from his own screenplay for Greenacre Films/UKFC and is also developing an original television series with the BBC.

Georgia Lowe | Set Designer

At the Finborough Theatre, Georgia was Set Designer for *Fanny and Faggot* (2007), *Follow* (2008) and *Blue Surge* (2011).

Studied at Exeter University and trained on the Motley Theatre Design Course. London. She is currently Trainee Designer at the Royal Shakespeare Company and was a finalist in the Linbury Prize for Stage Design 2011. Designs include *Amphibians* (Bridewell Theatre), *Yellow* (Riverside *Tete a Tete* Festival) *Drowning on Dry Land* (Jermyn Street Theatre), *Legacy Falls* (New Players Theatre), *Days of Hope, The Shadow Master, Lone Star/Private Wars* (King's Head Theatre), *Back of the Throat, Stephen and the Sexy Partridge* (Old Red Lion Theatre), *In My Name* (Trafalgar Studios), *I am Montana* (Arcola Theatre), *WORD:PLAY 2* (Theatre 503) and *Thin Toes* (Pleasance London), and she was Costume Designer for *Departure Lounge* (Waterloo East Theatre). She has also designed for a number of opera workshops including Dartington International Festival and the Jerwood Opera writing course in Aldeburgh, alongside Harrison Birtwistle, Stephen Langridge and Alison Chitty. Assisting credits include *The Merchant of Venice, A Midsummer Night's Dream, Marat/Sade, What Country Friends Is This?* (all for the Royal Shakespeare Company) and *Stovepipe* (Hightide).

Arnim Friess | Lighting Designer

At the Finborough Theatre, Arnim was Lighting Designer for *The Grapes of Wrath* (2000).

Trained at the Birmingham Institute of Art and Design. Theatre includes The *Death of Harry* (Ouroborus Theatre), *National Holocaust Memorial Day, Lucky Seven* (Hampstead Theatre), *Joe Guy* (Soho Theatre), *Looking for JJ* (Unicorn Theatre), *One Night in November, Monged, Puntila and His Man Matti, The Mysteries* (Belgrade Theatre, Coventry), *The Suicide,*

An Inspector Calls (Clwyd Theatr Cymru), *Mine* (National Tour),*The White Album* (Nottingham Playhouse), *The Pitchshifter* (for leading Dutch contemporary music ensemble Insomnia), *Rumblefish, Road, Lord of the Flies* (Pilot Theatre), *Amour* (Oval House Theatre and the Dance Centre, Toronto), *Moll Flanders, Metropolis, The Importance of Being Earnest* (Kaos Theatre), *Paradise* (Birmingham Rep), *Angels in America* (Crucible Theatre, Sheffield), *Oliver!* (Liverpool Playhouse), Mozart's *Mass in C Minor* (Birmingham Royal Ballet), *My Beautiful Launderette* (Snap Theatre), *The Wall, King, Satyagraha* (MAC Birmngham), *Shot Through the Heart* (Pentabus Theatre) and *Hard Day's Night* (Hull Truck Theatre Company). Other work includes the bricks-in-space spectacle *Life on Mars* at Legolands worldwide, and the appearance of hundreds of angels inside St Paul's Cathedral for the City of London Festival.

Rachel Szmukler | Costume Designer

At the Finborough Theatre, Rachel was Costume Designer for *Blue Surge* (2011).

Studied at the Glasgow School of Art and on the Motley Theatre Design Course, London. Theatre includes set and costume design for *Olly's Prison* (Cock Tavern), *Winter Tales* (Firstborn Theatre Company), *Semele* (Hampstead Garden Opera) and *The Writers' Room* (Tour), and set design for *The White House* (Courtyard Studio Theatre), as well as being Design Assistant for *Slick* (National Youth Theatre). Film includes costume design for *Strays* (National Film and Television School).

Edward Lewis | Sound Designer

At the Finborough Theatre, Edward was Sound Designer for *Vibrant – An Anniversary Festival of Finborough Playwrights* (2010), *In the Blood* (2010), *The December Man/L'homme de Décembre* (2011), *Accolade* (2011), *Bed and Sofa* (2011), *Beating Heart Cadaver* (2011), *Vibrant – A Festival of Finborough Playwrights* (2011), *Mirror Teeth* (2011), *Blue Surge* (2011), *Perchance to Dream* (2011), *Drama at Inish* (2011) and *Rigor Mortis* (2011).

Studied Music at Oxford University and subsequently trained as a composer and sound designer at the Bournemouth Media School. Theatre includes *On the Rocks, Amongst Friends, Darker Shores* (Hampstead Theatre), *Slowly, Hurts Given and Received, Apple Pie* (Riverside Studios), *Measure for Measure* (Sherman Cymru), *Emo* (Bristol Old Vic and Young Vic), *I Am Falling* (Sadler's Wells and Gate Theatre), *The Stronger, The Pariah, Boy with a Suitcase, Le Marriage and Meetings* (Arcola Theatre), *Hedda, Breathing Irregular* (Gate Theatre), *Madness in Valencia* (White Bear Theatre and Trafalgar Studios), *Orpheus and Eurydice* and *Quartet* (Old Vic Tunnels), *The Madness of George III* (National Tour), *Love, Question Mark* (New Diorama Theatre), *Knives in Hens* (BAC), *Personal Enemy* (White Bear Theatre and US tour), *Kalagora* (national and international tour), *Mad, Funny, Just, Mimi and the Stalker* (Theatre 503), *The London Plays* (Old Red Lion Theatre), *Cyrano de Bergerac, Bloody Poetry, Madman's Confession* (White Bear Theatre), *No Way Out* (Hen and Chickens Theatre), *Striking 12* (Waterloo East Theatre), *Heat and Light* (Hampstead Theatre), *Diary of a Madman* (Rosemary Branch Theatre), *The Death of Cool* (Tristan Bates Theatre) and *Full Circle* (Oval House Theatre), as well as on the Arden

Project for the Old Vic. He has recently been nominated for an Off West End Theatre Award, and films he has recently worked on have won several awards at the LA and Filmstock International Film Festivals.

Steve Medlin | Fight Director

At the Finborough Theatre, Steve was Movement Director for *Achidi J's Final Hours* (2004).

Trained as an actor and teacher at Rose Bruford College following study with David Glass and Théâtre de Complicité. Theatre includes *Winners* (Young Vic), *Urban Legend* (Liverpool Playhouse), *Obsessions* (Arts Theatre), *Indiana Jones and the Lost Kingdom* (Commonwealth Institute), *Glow* (Theatre Centre), *The Hounding of David Oluwale* (West Yorkshire Playhouse) and *One Monkey Don't Stop No Show* (Crucible Theatre, Sheffield). Television includes *Political Edge* and *Jungle Run*. Film includes *Sweeney Todd*.

Arezou Ali | Stage Manager

Studied at Soureh University, Tehran and the Central School of Speech and Drama. Theatre includes *Baggage, Horseplay* (Proud Gallery, Camden), *People You May Know* (Takeover Festival), *You Me Bum Bum Train* (Barbican Theatre), *Whose Cloud Is It Anyway?* (Central School of Speech and Drama), *Butterfly and Yoke* (Nuit Blanche Festival, Lucernaire Theatre, Paris), *What You Heard Is Instrument of Silence* (City Theatre, Tehran), *The Birdman of Mother's Garden* (City Theatre, Tehran), *Dingo Maro* (City Theatre, Tehran) and *7 Minutes 50 Seconds* (Vahdat Hall, Tehran).

Production Acknowledgements

Promotional Filming | Tom Middleton
Poster Design | Sean Butt

Special Thanks to

Cromiard Ltd, who would like their donation to *Fog* dedicated to the memory of Captain Alan Crompton, aged 27, of The Royal Engineers, who was sadly killed in a car crash in Suffolk on Saturday, 24 September: 'A natural leader and a true gentleman, in every sense of the word.'

The Royal Victoria Hall Foundation
Alan Rickman
Mark Rylance
Irene East
Pam Redican www.wingsschool.co.uk
The Actors Temple www.actorstemple.com
Benjamin Glean
Hannah Fairclough
Roy Williams OBE
Jane Fallowfield

FINBOROUGH | THEATRE

Winner – *London Theatre Reviews'* Empty Space Peter Brook Award 2010

'One of the most stimulating venues in London, fielding a programme that is a bold mix of trenchant, politically thought-provoking new drama and shrewdly chosen revivals of neglected works from the past.' *Independent*

'A disproportionately valuable component of the London theatre ecology. Its programme combines new writing and revivals, in selections intelligent and audacious.' *Financial Times*

'A blazing beacon of intelligent endeavour, nurturing new writers while finding and reviving neglected curiosities from home and abroad.' *Daily Telegraph*

Founded in 1980, the multi-award-winning Finborough Theatre presents plays and music theatre, concentrated exclusively on new writing and genuine rediscoveries from the 19th and 20th centuries. We offer a stimulating and inclusive programme, appealing to theatregoers of all generations and from a broad spectrum of the population. Behind the scenes, we continue to discover and develop a new generation of theatre makers – through our vibrant Literary Department, our internship programme, our Resident Assistant Director Programme and our partnership with the National Theatre Studio – the Leverhulme Bursary for Emerging Directors.

Despite remaining completely unfunded, the Finborough Theatre has an unparalleled track record of attracting the finest creative talent, as well as discovering new playwrights who go on to become leading voices in British theatre. Under Artistic Director Neil McPherson, it has discovered some of the UK's most exciting new playwrights including Laura Wade, James Graham, Mike Bartlett, Sarah Grochala, Jack Thorne, Simon Vinnicombe, Alexandra Wood, Al Smith, Nicholas de Jongh and Anders Lustgarten.

Artists working at the theatre in the 1980s included Clive Barker, Rory Bremner, Nica Burns, Kathy Burke, Ken Campbell, Jane Horrocks and Claire Dowie. In the 1990s, the Finborough Theatre became known for new writing including Naomi Wallace's first play *The War Boys*; Rachel Weisz in David Farr's *Neville*

Southall's *Washbag*; four plays by Anthony Neilson including *Penetrator* and *The Censor*, both of which transferred to the Royal Court Theatre; and new plays by Tony Marchant, David Eldridge, Mark Ravenhill and Phil Willmott. New writing development included a number of works that went to become modern classics including Mark Ravenhill's *Shopping and F***king*, Conor McPherson's *This Lime Tree Bower*, Naomi Wallace's *Slaughter City* and Martin McDonagh's *The Pillowman*.

Since 2000, new British plays have included Laura Wade's London debut *Young Emma*, commissioned for the Finborough Theatre; James Graham's *Albert's Boy* with Victor Spinetti; Sarah Grochala's *S27*; Peter Nichols' *Lingua Franca*, which transferred to Off-Broadway; and Joy Wilkinson's *Fair*; Nicholas de Jongh's *Plague Over England*; and Jack Thorne's *Fanny and Faggot*, all of which transferred to the West End. The late Miriam Karlin made her last stage appearance in *Many Roads to Paradise* in 2008. Many of the Finborough Theatre's new plays have been published and are on sale from our website.

UK premieres of foreign plays have included Brad Fraser's *Wolfboy*; Lanford Wilson's *Sympathetic Magic*; Larry Kramer's *The Destiny of Me*; Tennessee Williams' *Something Cloudy, Something Clear*; the English premiere of Robert McLellan's Scots language classic *Jamie the Saxt*; and three West End transfers – Frank McGuinness' *Gates of Gold* with William Gaunt and John Bennett, Joe DiPietro's *F***ing Men* and Craig Higginson's *Dream of the Dog* with Janet Suzman.

Rediscoveries of neglected work have included the first London revivals of Rolf Hochhuth's *Soldiers* and *The Representative*; both parts of Keith Dewhurst's *Lark Rise to Candleford*; *The Women's War*, an evening of original suffragette plays; Marlane Gomard Meyer's *Etta Jenks* with Clarke Peters and Daniela Nardini; Noël Coward's first play, *The Rat Trap*; Charles Wood's *Jingo* with Susannah Harker; Emlyn Williams' *Accolade* with Aden Gillett and Graham Seed; and Lennox Robinson's *Drama at Inish* with Celia Imrie and Paul O'Grady.

Music theatre has included the new (premieres from Grant Olding, Charles Miller, Michael John LaChuisa, Adam Guettel, Andrew Lippa and Adam Gwon's *Ordinary Days* which transferred to the West End) and the old (the UK premiere of Rodgers and Hammerstein's *State Fair* which also transferred to the West End, and the acclaimed Celebrating British Music Theatre series, reviving forgotten British musicals).

The Finborough Theatre won *London Theatre Reviews'* Empty Space . . . Peter Brook Award in 2010, the Empty Space . . . Peter Brook Awards Dan Crawford Pub Theatre Award in 2005 and 2008, the Empty Space Peter Brook Mark Marvin Award in 2004, and four awards in the inaugural 2011 Off West End Awards. It is the only theatre without public funding to be awarded the Pearson Playwriting Award bursary for writers Chris Lee in 2000, Laura Wade in 2005 (who also went on to win the Critics' Circle Theatre Award for Most Promising Playwright, the George Devine Award and an Olivier Award nomination), James Graham in 2006, Al Smith in 2007, Anders Lustgarten in 2009 and Simon Vinnicombe in 2010. Three bursary holders (Laura Wade, James Graham and Anders Lustgarten) have also won the Catherine Johnson Award for Best Play written by a bursary holder. Artistic Director Neil McPherson won the Best Artistic Director award from *Fringe Report* in 2009 and is nominated for the Off West End Awards in 2011, and a Writers' Guild Award for the Encouragement of New Writing in 2010.

www.finboroughtheatre.co.uk

FINBOROUGH | THEATRE

118 Finborough Road, London SW10 9ED
admin@finboroughtheatre.co.uk
www.finboroughtheatre.co.uk

The Leverhulme Bursary for Emerging Directors is a partnership between the National Theatre Studio and the Finborough Theatre, supported by The Leverhulme Trust.

The Finborough Theatre has the support of the Pearson Playwrights' Scheme. Sponsored by Pearson PLC.

The Finborough Theatre is a member of the Independent Theatre Council, Musical Theatre Matters UK (MTM:UK) and The Earl's Court Society www.earlscourtsociety.org.uk

Ecovenue is a European Regional Development Fund backed three year initiative of The Theatres Trust, aiming to improve the environmental sustainability of 48 small to medium sized performing arts spaces across London. www.ecovenue.org.uk

FINBOROUGH

The Finborough Wine Café
Contact Rob Malcolm or Monique Ziervogel on 020 7373 0745 or
finboroughwinecafe@gmail.com

Online
Join us at Facebook, Twitter, MySpace and YouTube.

Mailing
Email admin@finboroughtheatre.co.uk or give your details to our Box Office staff to
join our free email list. If you would like to be sent a free season leaflet every three
months, just include your postal address and postcode.

Feedback
We welcome your comments, complaints and suggestions. Write to Finborough
Theatre, 118 Finborough Road, London SW10 9ED or email us at admin@
finboroughtheatre.co.uk

Friends
The Finborough Theatre is a registered charity. We receive no public funding, and
rely solely on the support of our audiences. Please do consider supporting us by
becoming a member of our Friends of the Finborough Theatre scheme. There are four
categories of Friends, each offering a wide range of benefits.

Brandon Thomas Friends – Bruce Cleave. Mike Lewendon.
Richard Tauber Friends – Harry MacAuslan. Brian Smith.
William Terriss Friends – Leo and Janet Liebster. Philip Hooker. Peter Lobl. Bhagat
Sharma. Thurloe and Lyndhurst LLP. Jon Sedmak.

Smoking is not permitted in the auditorium and the use of cameras and recording
equipment is strictly prohibited.

In accordance with the requirements of the Royal Borough of Kensington and Chelsea:

1. The public may leave at the end of the performance by all doors and such doors must at that time
be kept open.
2. All gangways, corridors, staircases and external passageways intended for exit shall be left
entirely free from obstruction whether permanent or temporary.
3. Persons shall not be permitted to stand or sit in any of the gangways intercepting the seating or
to sit in any of the other gangways.

The Finborough Theatre is licensed by the Royal Borough of Kensington and Chelsea to The Steam
Industry, a registered charity and a company limited by guarantee. Registered in England no.
3448268. Registered Charity no. 1071304. Registered Office: 118 Finborough Road, London SW10
9ED. The Steam Industry is under the Artistic Direction of Phil Willmott. www.philwillmott.co.uk

Fog

Introduction

So, how did an actor in his twenties come to write a play like *Fog* with a sixty year old woman? It's the question most often asked. Especially as the woman was a founder member of Siren, a lesbian feminist theatre company that toured throughout the 1980s.

Back story – Tash was the partner of Toby's mother. For a teenage grime MC, mindful of his street cred, having a lesbian mum was a definite disadvantage, so relations with her partner were slow to warm up.

It took Toby's auditions to drama school, weeks of working together through extended Shakespearean metaphors and iambic pentameters, to forge a common bond. When it came to Toby's third-round audition to RADA, he was short of just the right modern piece. So they wrote one.

The RADA panel loved it, and wanted to read the whole play. Well, they already had a character and half a page of dialogue . . . so, *Fog* was born.

Unlike some co-writers who write whole chunks on their own, Toby and Tash have always written together, bouncing ideas off each other, improvising the scenes, and then honing each word, debating each comma and full stop. The big difference in age and experience, something that might have proved a handicap, only served to enrich the process and, of course, the play.

Characters

Fog, *male, white, 17 years old. Emotionally very damaged. Fairly tall, looks undernourished. Hair very short, if not shaven. Wears tracksuit bottoms or baggy jeans, with flash trainers, hoodie, and rosary round his neck. Normally speaks quite a thick urban black London dialect. Father put him in care when his mother died 10 years ago. Brother to Lou, son to Cannon.*

Cannon, *male, white, mid-forties. Tall, burly, getting a beer gut. Speaks a better class of cockney when he remembers to. Now an ex-army sergeant, he put the children in care shortly after his wife died, and returned to his regiment. He hasn't seen them since.*

Lou, *female, white, 20 years old. Quite striking looking. Wears sophisticated street clothes with style. Speaks a mixture of urban black and cockney. She was in care with Fog, and left at 18 for her own flat. She'd planned to have Fog live with her, but just couldn't hack being out of care and got into drugs and crime and went to prison for a while.*

Michael, *black, male 18 years old. Dresses and speaks street but, having done well at school, has gained the label of 'boffin'. Friend of Fog from early childhood. Really Fog's only friend. Brother to Bernice.*

Bernice, *female, black, 24 years old. Her accent varies according to situation. Smartly dressed. Has ambition, having worked her way up in the same firm leaving school. She particularly has ambition for Michael.*

Scene One

Stage dark. Off-stage, light goes on, then goes off.

Fog   Wossat?

Cannon   Bulb . . . or fuse. We'll see.

We hear **Cannon** *and* **Fog** *enter. Light goes on onstage. The council flat is littered with the kind of stuff a family with small children might leave behind. Articles must include a battered tricycle and an old armchair.*

Cannon *sighs.*

Fog   Yeaaahh!

Cannon   Yeah.

Fog   Oh my!

Cannon *sighs more audibly.*

Fog   Dis is . . . / dis is . . .

Cannon   Uh huh.

Fog   Eyy, look at . . . (*To window, which is the audience.*) Oh! Oy a balcony!

Cannon   Right. Don't worry, boy, I'll sort this.

He gets out mobile phone.

Fog   Bwoy! Top floor!

Cannon   And I ain't takin no for an answer.

Dialling and redialling during the next piece of dialogue.

Fog   Can't get better than that! Without being on the roof.

Cannon   I've earned a bloody garden. It's the least they can give me.

Fog (*exploring offstage. Distant light goes on*)   Yes, dese work.

Cannon   A garden flat. Is that really too much to ask for from this . . .?

Fog   Oy, it's got one . . .

Cannon (*still trying to get through on phone*)   . . . fuckin' country? / Ey?

Fog (*still off*)   . . . two . . . three . . .

Cannon   And, while we're at it, just a little bit of . . .

Fog   Four rooms!

Cannon   Respect would be nice.

Fog (*re-appearing*)   Counting the toilet. Could I like have da one next ta . . . to uhm . . .

Cannon (*still trying on his mobile*)   Wha'?

Fog   Can I have dat one, please?

Cannon   What?

Fog   Can I have that one? / Please.

Cannon   What, you like it?

Fog   Yeah.

Cannon   No, you don't.

Fog   I do.

Cannon   You wanna live 'ere? You don't wanna live 'ere.

Fog   I do.

Cannon   You wanna live 'ere?

Fog   Yeah.

Cannon (*puts away phone*)   What about the garden?

Fog   Iss downstairs.

Cannon   But it's not our garden. I thought you'd want a garden.

Fog   I'm fine, thanks.

Cannon   But a garden . . . where you can play? Or 'ave a kickabout? Look, we're not going to settle for just anything. I am owed big time, OK?

Fog   OK.

Cannon   That's right. That's right. Because, this is not what I had in mind for us. I wanna make this a proper home.

Fog   Can we put the telly dere?

Cannon   Ey?

Fog   Can we put the telly dere, please. By the window. But not like . . . like screwed to the wall, not up high?

Cannon   What?

Fog   And can we have . . . Dad? . . . can we have plasma?

Cannon   If you want it you'll get it.

Fog   'Cos you have to have them in England now anyway.

Cannon   Right. (*Looking round.*) Pigsty.

Fog   Yeah, yeah I fink it's da law.

Cannon   What is?

Fog   Digital plasma.

Cannon   Right. Alright then. If it's what you want . . .?

Fog   Yeah.

Cannon (*sighs*)   Your Mum would've known how to do it. She'd've made this home in a minute. All those little touches she used to do . . . OK. Right. Yeah, get rid of all this shit. Disinfect, top to bottom. Fill those holes in. Proper paint job. Simple, I can. If it's what you want . . . But, just comin' up in the lift, it's / disgustin'.

Fog   Nah nah nah, lift was fine. Just *smelt* like piss.

Cannon   Yeah, and looked like piss, 'cos it is piss, right up the fuckin' walls it's piss!

Fog   Nah, iss a chemical in the metal. To stop it breaking down.

Cannon   I want to give you something more than this.

Fog   But da lifts never break down.

Cannon   And as for them drug addicts on the landing!

Fog   Nah, dey're just little boys.

Cannon   Doing drugs.

Fog   Yeah, but I fink it's legal now anyway.

Cannon   Fuck legal, you're doin' nuffin'. You ain't pissing round with no drug dealers.

Fog (*fast*)   Who says?

Cannon   Ey?

Fog   Who says . . . who says dey're dealers? Dere ain't no shotters on dis block. Dat's why I like it.

Cannon   Because drugs fuck you up. OK?

Fog   Dat's why I like it. Dad.

Cannon   Good man. Good man.

Fog (*moving to front of stage*)   Ey, you can see everyt'ing from here.

Fog *surveys his world and* **Cannon** *looks at his son.*

Fog   Brock 'Ouse.

Cannon   Yeah? (*Moving to window.*)

Fog   Yeah, there.

Cannon   Ah, you can see right across the river. Look, Canary Wharf. Tell you what, we could go up there. Top floor. 'Ave a look through the telescopes.

Fog   Bye bye, Brock House. Used to stand at my window and look up 'ere, . . . now I'm standing up 'ere, looking dere.

Cannon   Yeah, it's been a tough time. But it's all over now. Forget about Brock House. All over now. We forget that. Start again. You, me and your sister.

Fog   Nah.

Cannon   Ey?

Fog   Nah. Not her.

Cannon   Well of course her.

Fog   She's gone.

Cannon   Yeah I know that, but she can't of gone far.

Fog   I told ya. She's gone.

Cannon   No, she ain't *gone*. Gone is gone, but she's somewhere.

Fog   Nah.

Cannon   And they know where, that's what gets me. Data protection! I'm her father, for fuck's sake. I'll find her.

Fog   You won't.

Cannon   Why?

Fog   'Cos you won't. Anyway, I don't care.

Cannon   Something happen wiv you two?

Fog   What?

Cannon   Did you fall out?

Fog   Nah.

Cannon   Nah, go on. What happened?

Fog   Forget it.

Cannon   Don't you tell me to forget it. I thought she was looking after you. She was supposed to look after you.

Fog   She definite didn't do that.

Cannon   Alright I get that, so tell me / what happened.

Fog   It's cool. I handled it.

Cannon   Look I don't want you two quarrelling.

Fog   Ey, man can see all o' de estate from here. Da whole territory.

Cannon   Whatever it was, it's done now. No grudges. We're starting over. Clean sheet.

Fog   Man can see all o' you

Watch it now what ya do

Keep my eye spy on you

Open wide so you can't hide,

Cannon   No stop talking / daft.

Fog   I can see right inside . . . you, Tennyson Tower! I see ya, Shelley. Yeah, ya can cover all da balconies from 'ere. 'Cept Wordsworth.

(*To* **Cannon**.) Oi! Is dis where you'd put sniper?

Cannon   What?

Fog   Place da man wi' da sub?

Cannon   What you talkin' 'bout now?

Fog   In the war zone.

Cannon   What war zone?

Fog   Like dis is a war zone, ya get me? An' we gotta take 'em all out, see?

Fog *is pointing to opposite balconies.*

Fog   Like dere . . . dere . . . dere . . . / dere . . .

Cannon   Right right. OK. Strategically speaking, well let's see . . . Yeah yeah, it's a pretty good vantage point, I guess. But double-edged. They could pick you off just as easy. Look, son, why don't I take you back and pick up / your stuff?

Fog (*machine-gunning explosively out the window*)   Da-da-da-da-da-da-da-da-da . . .!

Cannon   Stop that! Stop it!! OK . . . don't wanna hold it down there, mate, or you'll have no balls left. Bring it up chest high, right up, right up, like this. See?

Fog *swings round to face* **Cannon**, *both are holding 'machine guns'.*

Blackout.

Scene Two

Cannon *and* **Fog** *clear the mess, leaving only armchair and tricycle. They get a suitcase and a few holdalls, then drag in paint tins, brushes, rollers, etc. and a decorator's trestle table on a couple of painting sheets. Fog sits on the trike switching channels on an imaginary remote while he stares at a blank wall.*

Fog   Forty-two inches. Izzat like dis wide . . . nah, like like dis wide?

Cannon   It's one yard six inches, old money.

Fog   Uh?

Cannon   You chose it.

Fog   I forgot.

Cannon   It's from where you are to . . . about that case.

Fog   Shit! Das proper wide.

Cannon   I hope you ain't gonna become a couch potata.

Fog   Plasmaaaah. Michael ain't got no plasma. Manz gonna get proper jealous, boy. (*Laughs to himself.*)

Cannon   Who's Michael then? A mate of yours?

Fog   Yeah. One of da man dem, ennit. Got my own cinema now, boy.

Cannon   What, is he from the home?

Fog   Brock 'Ouse? (*Laughs.*)

Cannon   What? What's funny?

Fog   Michael? From Brock 'Ouse! Man wouldn't survive a day.

Cannon   What?

Fog   Yeah, I like dat!

Cannon   Wasselike?

Fog   Ey?

Cannon   Michael.

Fog   Yeah.

Cannon   What?

Fog   Yeah, cool.

Cannon   That's no answer. What's he actually like?

Fog (*'switching channels'*)   MTV Cribs, I'm watchin' ya. I know where you live . . . (*Switch.*) . . . fuckin' Dragon Ball Z, wha' ya playin' at, rude boy? . . . (*Switch.*) . . . Channel U – I'm up there soon wi' my video. Fuck it! (*Switch.*)

Cannon   Look, if you don't like nothing, why are we getting one?

Fog   What?

Cannon   It's costing me a grand, mate. Why are we getting a telly if you don't like the programmes?

Fog   Uh?

Cannon   You 'eard.

Fog   Ca . . . ca man can't not 'ave a telly.

Cannon   Why not? We had satellite out there and I've hardly watched a thing in the last ten years.

Fog   Is it? 'Oo won last *Big Brother*?

Cannon   'Ow the fuck should I know?

Fog   Alright alright, OK, what about . . . what about in *EastEnders* then . . . who do you think / killed . . .?

Cannon   I told ya, I don't watch it.

Fog   Boy, das mad! Dat is mad! I know ten times . . . a hundred more fings den you.

Cannon   Yeah, and what things?

Fog   What . . . ya want me ta tell ya?

Cannon   Nah that's what I'm sayin, I don't care. None of it's worth knowing. (*Beat.*) You see what I'm saying?

Silence. **Fog** *switches channels.*

Fog   Dere s'pposed ta deliver it now. If man had credit I'd be on da phone, askin'.

Cannon   It's still early.

Fog *kicks one of the cases.*

Cannon   They said before two, it's only . . . twelve-o-five.

Fog (*quickly gets up*)   Manz gonna kick. I got shit to do.

Cannon   Nah nah, 'old on. It's your telly, you stay and wait for it. Patience is a virtue, mate. Something you learn out there. You'll be sitting on your arse for hours and hours, suddenly you got a firefight on your hands.

Fog   For real?

Cannon   Well yeah.

Fog   How many people you killed?

Cannon (*beat*)   Don't ever ask me that.

Silence.

Cannon   I got it! Oy listen listen. Why don't I get us tickets? Home game? Down the Emirates. (*No response.*) Oi, don't fuck about.

'Who to?

Who to be?

Who to be a . . .

Gooner?!'

Fog *returns to switching imaginary stations.*

Cannon   Come on, mate, you remember. Don't you?

Fog   Nah.

Cannon   Don't yer remember?

Fog   Shall we ring da TV people?

Cannon   Yer first game, mate? Arsenal 3 Blackburn 1? Oi, come on, what about the T-shirt then! You gotta remember that. Like yesterday, me. We come out the ground, yeah? Round the corner, Highbury tube yeah, the stall? And you standing there pointing at it. The Ian Wright T-shirt! Don't tell me you don't remember that? 'Ad 'is face printed on the front?

No response.

Cannon   And I got it for you, didn't I? Fuckin' cost me enough. It was worth every penny for the look on your face. Yeah?

No response.

Cannon   You loved that T-shirt . . . You still got it?

Fog   Nah.

Cannon   Always filthy. Wore it like a skin. Yeah. Yeah. Fuckin' hell. Like yesterday.

Cannon *watches* **Fog** *sucking the crucifix of the rosary around his neck.*

Cannon   Yep! Gonna have to clean up in 'ere. Make it nice and homely. Put some pictures of your mum on the wall.

Yeah. I was thinking I might build a book shelf. Get some books. Get down to some reading.

Silence.

Catholic ennit? Yeah, a lot of the men out there turned to religion. That or porn. Or both. No, but serious, helped them fight. I mean I'm not a believer myself, but I respect a man who is. Definitely. So when did all this happen?

Fog *looks at him.*

Cannon   I mean, good on yer. If it keeps you out of harm's way – sweet. Go on, let's have a look.

Fog   What dis? Man got it from shop. For fashion.

Cannon   Oh. Right.

Fog *fiddles with his mobile.*

Cannon   Texting a mate?

Fog   Nah.

Cannon   Why don't you give wassit . . . uh, Mike a ring?

Fog   Michael.

Cannon   Michael. Michael? Hold on, yeah. Yeah, that black kid. Wassit, mum was a . . .? Yeah she was a nurse. Lovely girl. Yeah yeah. Ask him over. 'Cos you know yer mates are always welcome. I mean, 'course they are, goes without sayin'. This is your home. Your real, proper home, I mean. Ey?

Fog   Yeah.

Cannon   So you can have who yer want. Yeah?

Fog   Yeah.

Cannon   Oi, oi, an' if you 'ave a bird round, remember, you got your own fucking room. Shut the door!

He laughs.

Yeah, we're good. We're all set up. We're alright. We just need ya sister.

Beat. He stands up.

I'm gonna go back down there and I'm gonna speak to the man in charge. Go straight to the top, sort this out once and for all. She can't of just dropped out the fuckin / system!!

Fog   Yeah I remember.

Cannon   Wha'?

Fog   T-shirt.

Cannon   Yeah? What do you remember?

Fog   Yeah.

Cannon   Go on. What do you remember?

Fog   Ian Wright.

Cannon   That's it. Go on.

Fog   'Ad his face on.

Cannon   Yes. That's the one!

They look at each other.

Scene Three

Cannon *and* **Fog**'s *flat.* **Fog**'s *hoodie, trainers and one sock are on the floor.* **Cannon** *is shining his shoes.* **Fog** *picks up cigarette from packet on table, lights it, turns on TV and changes channels.* **Cannon** *watches.*

Cannon   Midday. I've had a jog, picked up the paper. Yeah, there's a few jobs in there would suit my credentials. I've been down the laundrette. I didn't know if you wanted anything washed, because you were asleep. (*Watches* **Fog** *smoke.*) Cigarette before breakfast?

Fog *goes on changing channels.*

Cannon   No college today?

No response.

Cannon   I said, no college today?

Fog   No.

Cannon   So what are your plans?

Fog   I don't know.

Cannon   You don't know?

Fog   Nope.

Cannon   It's midday and you still don't know what you're doing.

Fog   I might check a couple people.

Cannon   Check a couple people.

Fog   Sort out some business.

Cannon   Oh, OK. And no homework?

Fog   Nah. Why you askin'?

Cannon   Because I'm your dad. That's what dads do. I always had homework.

Fog   Oh. Well yeah, it's not like that at mine.

Cannon   What do you mean?

Fog   Well, it's all hands-on. Studio. With the instruments.

Cannon   Well, if it's hands-on, boy, why ain't you there?

Fog   'Ca they're doin' the simple stuff right now. I got previous experience.

Cannon   Never hurts to go back to basics. That's what my dad always said.

Fog   Yeah but man's been in studio from day one. I started on da computer.

Cannon   Oh computer? That's one up on me. Yeah that's good. Looks good on a CV, computer. So in the end, what will you actually get from this?

Fog   What you mean?

Cannon   I mean, what's the qualification?

Fog   Producer.

Cannon   OK. Go on.

Fog   MC producer.

Cannon   Ey?

Fog   MC producer.

Cannon   And what's that?

Fog   Spittin'.

Cannon   Spitting?

Fog   On the mike.

Cannon   What?

Fog   Layin' down your beats.

Cannon   And this'll give you a proper living?

Fog   Yeah, 'course.

Cannon   Proper wage?

Fog   Yeah, all dat all dat.

Cannon   I mean, enough to live on?

Fog   Yes.

Cannon   Good. Good. Because you need to be looking to the future. Can't let it all slip away. Happens far too easy in this life. You know?

Fog   Yeah.

Cannon   You can drift along thinking you got all the time in the world. And suddenly it's all gone.

No response.

Can't let that happen, mate. Ey?

Fog   Nah.

Cannon   I just don't want it to happen to you.

Fog *drifts out the room.*

Cannon   Where you going?

Fog   I dunno.

Cannon (*under his breath*)   Fuck's sake.

He gets out a cigarette.

Fog (*off*)   Ah fuck!

Cannon   What? What?

Fog   Fuck, man.

He re-enters.

Cannon   What? What's the matter?

Fog   I left it.

Cannon   Left what?

Fog   Super Mario. My Mario.

Cannon   Mario?

Fog   Brock 'Ouse. My game.

Cannon   Game? Oh right.

Fog   My Mario! I left it Brock 'Ouse.

Cannon   Well, that's no problem. We'll pop back sometime and get it.

Fog   Nah, dem boys'll have it, Jason'll have it. Dat was my game, / man.

Cannon   Don't worry about it.

Fog   I loved that game now I ain't never gonna get it back.

Cannon   Alright we'll go and get it now then.

Fog   Nah, dem boys won't give it back.

Cannon   No. *I* will get it back, don't you worry. Alright?

Fog   Yeah.

Cannon   Well, go on then. Get some layers on.

Fog   And you'll sort it?

Cannon   Yeah, we're going now.

Fog   Yeah. Alright, dad.

Scene Four

Loud burst of pirate station fills the theatre, playing grime tune, with a couple of MCs going back to back. Cue for **Cannon** *to move his furniture from acting space.* **Michael** *enters and he and* **Fog** *arrange the furniture for* **Michael**'s *sitting room. Must include TV, two comfy armchairs and coffee table, on which there are some textbooks and* **Fog**'s *spliff-making stuff. Their ashtray is an empty Coke can.* **Michael** *lights up half a spliff, watched by* **Fog**.

Michael   What, traffic lights?

Fog   Yeah. I'm on dat, blud, I'm on dat.

The game is to inhale, hand the spliff on, hold your breath till it's handed back to you, repeat till end of spliff. They play, delaying the return of the spliff, laughing and coughing.

Fog   Oi. Oi my weed. My weed is potent! You know man's gonna be top shottah. Big man sorted me out, blud.

Michael   What, Simeon?

Fog   Yeah.

Michael   Simeon? For real?

Fog   Yeah yeah, me and him are cool now, blud. I'm one of his soldiers now, ya get me.

Michael   Heavy.

Fog   Yeah man. Sorted me nine bar of punk, zed of barley. Two grand flat. I'm on my way. To da future.

Michael   That's heavy.

Fog   Yeah, you'll see. Two months, man's gonna be stacking his collateral, boy.

Michael   Gonna be rolling, yeah?

Fog   Yeah, you'll see, when I pull up in my whip. Beep beep! BM. Audi TT. Jump in, drive ya round the block. (**Michael** *laughs*.) Ya like dat, innit?

Fog *turning into MC with Jamaican accent.*

   White boy turn top shottah

Holds pretend gun in the air.

   Gonnin' a' di air
   Deal widdit propah,
   Dis is da white boy shottah.

Tiny pause.

   Got my trainer from Foot Locker!

Michael (*laughing*)   Yeah, man.

Fog   Yeah!

Michael   Yeah yeah.

Fog (*in strong Jamaican accent*)   Pretty boy! All de gal dem want *you*.

Michael   Shut up, man.

Fog   Got bare gels now, ennit? All want a bit of Michael. *My* boy, ya get me?

Beat.

What what what?!

'Fink you're a big boy

'Cos you got a tash?

(*Together.*) Bullets'll catch your face like a rash!

Michael   That lighter's sick, blud.

Fog   Yeah man, my dad's, ennit.

Michael   Yeah, got your dad back now?

Fog   Yeah, it's good, blud! Milton Heights. Ya get me.

Michael   T'ings are changing for you.

Fog   Top floor, blud.

Michael   On you're way now.

Fog   Top floor! Milton Heights.

Michael   Yeah man, movin' up.

Fog   Dassit, I'm movin' up.

Michael   So wass he sayin'?

Fog   Who?

Michael   Your dad.

Fog   Telescopic vision, blud. Night sight 'fra red.

Michael   What?

Fog   He let me hold it, blud. Up 'ere. He showed me. It's how you hold it, blud. See? (*On feet, moving forward.*) Out ta da balcony, ta di advantage point . . . movin' quiet, no sound, no need, know da drill, get it in my night sight . . . bang! Took out da dog!

Michael *laughs.*

Fog   Lootenant Colonel Cannon.

Michael   Who dat? Yer dad?

Fog   Nah, me, blud, me. Royal Marine, fuckin' . . . SAS
Para, ya get me? Ya don't fuck wid da SAS in da killin' fields,
blud. Mark my words.

'Permission to leave, sir? For da sake of my motherless kids.'

'Permission . . . not permitted, soldier.'

When you're Lootenant Colonel, see, they don't fuckin' let
you go! Dass da t'ing. Dass da t'ing! Man's been dere every
time. Ev-er-y time! Vietnam . . . fuckin' . . . fuckin' . . .

Michael   Bosnia?

Fog   Yes!

Michael   Iraq?

Fog   Yeah, all o' dem tings blud, all o' dem.

Bernice *enters, carrying two forks, two plates and a bag of
takeaway.*

Bernice   Got a posh Chinese! (*Looking at* **Michael**.) To
celebrate! Oh, hello Bernice. Dat's nice, Bernice. And why
are we celebrating, Bernice? Well, Michael, thanks for
asking. The answer to your question is because I am so on
the way to promotion. Your big sister is going to be the next
Manager, South East Division!

Michael   Seen.

Bernice   This is big time, Michael! This is Oxford for you.
You get me?

Michael   I told you, I ain't.

Bernice   Nah nah nah. You are going.

Michael *shakes his head.*

Bernice   Anyway, I digress. Yeah, I had no suspicion of it.
That's the weird thing. It was just a normal morning. (*She
begins to lay out takeaway on the coffee table.*) Read my emails,
did my figures, passed them on to Margot, blah blah blah –

early, as always, then at 10.28 – flagging it up – Janice says
– told you about Janice, didn't I? Husband snores and keeps
dying in his sleep.

(*To* **Fog** *whose leg is stretched out in front of her.*) 'Scuse me.
Excuse me. (**Fog** *moves leg.*) Thank you – she says let's go for
our break now. So, we're nearly out the door when . . . what
happens? The phone rings. Leave it, says Janice. No, I can't,
I say. Just my luck it'll be Vince and it's still only . . . keep up,
Michael . . .

Michael   10.28.

Bernice (*nice French accent*)   Exactement. Peking roast
duck. King prawns. So I pick up. 'Hello, Sales and Services,
Bernice speaking. How can I help you?' And Vince says,
'You can help me by coming to my office immediately,
Bernice.' Mi-chael, my whole life passed before me . . . Nah,
hold on. What are you doing?

Michael   I'm giving him some prawn crackers.

Bernice   Two plates? Two forks? Two people.

Michael   He can have some of mine.

Bernice   Nah, nah, I'm not some charity.

Michael   Bee, I ain't even that hungry.

Bernice   I don't care, Michael. He ain't having none of
my food.

Fog (*muttering*)   Don't even want any . . .

Bernice   Always come beggin' and slouchin' up the place.
And, what the fuck is he even doing here anyway, when
you're meant to be studying?

Michael   I've done what I need to do.

Bernice   Oh really.

Michael   Yes, really.

Fog   He's been reading.

Bernice   Yeah? Yeah? And you've been helping, have you?

Fog   Yeah, 'course.

Bernice   Oh, whatever!

Fog   Yeah, whatever.

Bernice   It's your life anyway.

Michael   Ah, come on. Forget all that.

Bernice   And the house all stinking up of weed.

Michael   Come, I wanna hear what happened?

Bernice   Shuttup.

Michael   Come on.

Bernice   No. You're not interested.

Michael   I am, man! 'Course I am. Go on.

Bernice   Alright. So, down I go. To see Vince.

Michael   Yeah.

Bernice   I knock at the door, heartbeat banging so loud you can hear it all the way down the corridor, 'Come in.' Breathe, Bernice, breathe. Open the door, there's Vince with Mrs Barforth, Human Resources, *and*, wait for it, Mr Harrison The Sales Director, South East! Like . . . you know?

Michael   Yeah.

Bernice   So now I'm just a puddle on the floor, and Vince says, 'Sit down, Bernice.' And you can't read Vince, that's the thing. Shuffles papers. Coughs. Frowns. And I'm thinking, well why not just fucking shoot me now? Put me out my misery. Then he starts, 'We have been reviewing your progress over the last five years, and we have come to . . . *a very favourable impression*!'

Michael   Wow!

Bernice   And then he goes, yeah, . . . what was it? 'We consider you an asset to the company, Bernice.' Asset! So then Mr Harrison – ah he's got the most beautiful blue eyes, Michael, sort of amethyst you know – he goes, 'This is strictly within these walls, Bernice, but Allison Mitchell is moving to our Luxembourg office in September, so her post will become vacant.' Michael?

Michael   Yeah, vacant.

Bernice   Yeah. 'And we would like someone of *your calibre* to fill it!'

Michael   Shit! So yer got the job?

Bernice   Hang on. So then he looks at Mrs Barforth – Human Resources –

Michael   Yeah, yeah.

Bernice   Yeah, who says, 'Of course, we are an equal opportunities employer, Bernice,' – first I'd heard of it, – 'so we do have to advertise the position'.

Michael   What, so you haven't got the job?

Bernice   Yeah. No. Well, what I mean is . . . what she's implying is . . . See, they have got to go through the 'procedures', don't they? (*Her mobile rings*.) Wassup, Shan? I know! I know, I still can't believe it! Oy but thinking about it now – (*To* **Michael**.) do not open them till I'm back! – ah Shan, I can see the signs all over da place. (*Exits talking*.) This morning! 10.28 – flagging it up – Janice says – I told you about Janice, didn't I? Yeah, I did. Husband . . .

Michael *slumps back down again.*

Fog   She talks shit, man.

Michael   Oi.

Fog   She needs to know who she's fuckin' talkin' to.

Michael   Yeah, whatever.

Fog   She can't go round talking like dat.

Michael   Shuttup.

Fog   Dass how you get shot round here, blud. I wouldn't do it 'cos she's your sister but ya need to / know dat.

Michael   You need to shut up now, bruv.

Fog   Nah, when I'm ready, bruv. When I'm ready.

Michael *doesn't respond.*

Fog   I ain't ready yet.

Michael *doesn't respond.*

Fog   Yeah, I'm ready now.

Michael *picks up one of the books, ignoring* **Fog**.

Fog   Oy . . . Professor Michael . . . big boy professor . . . ya get me? Ya get me, blud?

Blud?

Michael   I don't know any more.

Fog   What?

Michael   I don't even know, man.

Fog   What?

Michael   I dunno.

Fog   Talk, man.

Michael   I just . . . I dunno.

Fog   Talk.

Michael   Boy, it's mad . . . it's gonna be mad.

Fog   What is?

Michael (*beat*)   I really don't know. There's a lot of me that ain't feelin' to go. I mean – Oxford! It's just it's a . . .

Fog   What?

Michael   It's a different place.

Fog   Yeah.

Michael   Different faces.

Fog   Yeah white faces.

Michael   Mm.

Fog   Mm . . . Yeah. Yeah, all dem posh student ones!

Michael   Yeah, exactly.

Fog   Blazin' up in their rooms. Needing supply. Bare customers. Bwoy, we'll be runnin' shit up there.

Michael   It's Oxford, man. It's way out the manor.

Fog   Nah nah, man'll drive you there. Audi TT, blacked out windows, suited and booted, lookin' all mysterious, ya get me? Bare chicks'll be clockin' us. Who dem boys? Who dem boys?

Michael   It ain't like that there.

Fog   'Course it is.

Michael   Nah, dem kind of girls don't go for that.

Fog   What, they go for a skinny white posh boy yeah?

Michael   I dunno.

Fog   What, they don't go for the hardness that we bring? Man dem from road, you get me. They won't know what's hit dem!

Michael   Ah whatever, I dunno. It's all bullshit, anyway, ennit. Man don't need dat kinda stress.

Fog   True true true true. Man needs time to relax a bit. Chill with his boys.

Michael   Dassit. Thank you. Thank you. Uni ain't the only t'ing out there.

Fog (*beat*)   Yeah, but dat's your t'ing, blud. You was born boffin.

Michael   Shuttup.

Fog   Nah, dass what you're meant to do. You love all dat.

Michael   Yeah but, still . . .

Fog   Nah, still nothing. Nothing, y'understand? You know?

Michael   What?

Fog   You know.

Michael   What?

Fog   Just don't be scared. Blud?

Michael   Yeah.

Fog   Anyway, I'll be there. I got your back.

Michael   Yeah?

Fog   'Course.

Bernice *re-enters, still on the phone.*

Bernice   Mm mm, I know. Hold up, Shan. (*To* **Fog**.) Are you still here? Will you give him a break? Can you not see he's trying to study? Michael, can you tell your friend to leave now?

Blackout.

Scene Five

Change into **Cannon** *and* **Fog***'s flat. TV remains from last scene. Another old armchair is added. The painting stuff is put in the same position except for the decorator's trestle that now serves as a coffee table. The programme* Dragon Ball Z *is playing loud on the TV.* **Cannon** *enters, goes to TV, turns it off.*

Fog (*re-entering on the tricycle*)   It ain't finished yet.

Cannon   What?

Fog   TV.

Cannon   Yes, it has. Well, ain't you going to ask?

Fog   What?

Cannon   Interview. If you can call it that! You know what I
mean? You know what I mean?

Fog   Yeah.

Cannon   Yeah, I don't know who the fuck they thought I
was. Some fuckin' . . . bollocks . . . I shouldn't 'ave bothered.
Waste of time, mate, start to finish.

Looks at **Fog** *whose hand is straying to remote.*

Cannon   You know?

Fog   Yeah.

He fiddles with remote but without picking it up.

Cannon   I told 'em. Told 'em straight. Security, I said? You
gotta be joking. This ain't security. I've *forgotten* more about
security than they'll ever know. You know what I mean?

Again looking at **Fog**.

Fog   Yeah yeah.

Cannon   Yeah. Waste of time. All of it. Waste of fuckin' time.
I mean, what's goin' on here, ey? What's goin' on here for
Christ's sake?

Fog *puts down the remote.*

Cannon   Fuckin' Mickey Mouse country or what! Ey?

Fog   Yeah, man.

Cannon   And look at this fuckin' place, ey? Look at it.
Fuckin' . . . Fuck's sake! I need to get out. I need to get out
or I'm gonna . . . OK . . . OK let me just . . . just . . . OK . . .
OK . . .

Fog *is very still.*

Cannon   Yes. Yes, you're right, we should get out. Go for a
walk.

Fog   Go for a drive.

Cannon   Thassit. Go buy a football, go up the park.

Fog Yeah, yeah.

Cannon Yeah?

Fog Yeah.

Cannon Yeah, that's it. We'll go for a walk by the river. Have a drink. What's that pub? Down by the river? That pub we . . .

Couple beats.

Cannon Nah, mate, this is gettin'. . . fuckin' . . . beyond a . . . can't have this. Need some. . . I need some space. Gotta get out!

Fog Go for a drive.

Cannon 12k a year! What can you do with that? Small change, small fuckin' change. Go private, I can earn that in a month. That's what they're getting out there.

Fog What . . . what are ya gonna go back?

Cannon Aegis. That's who they've all gone with. Aegis.

Fog But you're not going back?

Cannon Aegis'd snap me up. Snap me up like that.

Fog Are you? You're not going back, are you?

Cannon Ey? Nah mate. No. No 'course not. I mean I'm just sayin'. I'm just saying that's all, what can you do with 12k a year?

Fog We could get a car.

Cannon Ey?

Fog Ride round the block.

Cannon Oh yeah, yeah we could get a fuckin' car.

Fog We could get a car to da river.

Cannon Oh yeah we could, couldn't we?

Fog   Yes! And could we ride round London like, bare petrol? Get a BM, beep it out.

Cannon   Oh, of course, mate. I'll just go and pick up my wages, shall I?

Fog   Yeah, man!

Cannon   Yeah, why not?

Fog   An' you could teach me . . . if we had a car . . . you could teach me on it. If we had a car . . .

Cannon   You wanna car, yeah?

Fog   Yeah.

Cannon   Yeah?

Fog   Yes!

Cannon   I'll give you a car!

Cannon *goes straight for* **Fog** *and pushes him on the trike as fast as it will go.*

Cannon   Beep beep! Beep beep!

He pushes until he's out of breath then stops as abruptly as he started, leaving **Fog** *upstage and facing upstage on the tricycle.*

Cannon   There ya go. There's your car.

He muzzes up **Fog**'s *hair and moves to front of stage, looks out over balcony. Takes out a cigarette.* **Fog** *remains in same position.*

Fog   So what about the car?

Cannon, *his back to* **Fog**, *lights cigarette, inhales and exhales.*

Cannon   Hm?

Fog *gets up off tricycle, hooks one foot under seat and topples it over.*

Fog   The car?

Cannon   The car? Oh yeah. One day. (*Beat.*) You know what I was thinking of just now? Saint Mary's Bay. Your mum

loved that place. Real family place. Still got the pictures.
All us on the beach. Magic. Down the Kit Kat Cafe of an
evening. Toasted bacon sandwich and . . . wassit, what's that
ice cream in the big uhm . . .

Fog   Knickerbocker glory.

Cannon   Knickerbocker glory . . . thassit. Smashing. We
should all . . . . . we should . . . Where's my fuckin' daughter?
She should be here with us. Where is she? Ey? You don't
know I don't know no one seems to fuckin' know, or care.
What is wrong here? You could die in the fuckin' gutter and
no one cares. She could be . . . No, no she's somewhere.

Fog   She's gone, dad.

Cannon   Shut up I know she's gone.

Fog   She left the country.

Cannon   What?

Fog   Said she's never coming back.

Blackout.

Scene Six

Michael *and* **Bernice**'s *flat.* **Bernice** *sits in the middle of* **Lou**
and **Michael**, *who are in mid-conversation.*

Michael   Ah, Little Richie, man . . .

Lou   Yeah, first person I saw, coming back. Ain't seen him
in years.

Michael   Yeah, he don't change. Still gets in beef.

Lou   Ah, but he's so sweet!

Michael   Yeah, gentle giant, man. But heads see his height
and wanna step to him.

Lou   Ah, that ain't fair.

Michael   Nah, don't worry, he's got a tough fist.

Lou   Yeah.

Michael   Yes.

Lou (*looking round the room*)   Looks just the same, ya know. It's always felt so homey.

Michael   So how you been?

Lou   Great. Ya know. Lot's happening.

Michael   Ah, that's good, man. That's great.

Lou   Yeah, things just really moving now.

Michael   Ah nice so what's going on?

Lou   Well, I'm really chasing a job don't care what it is. Just till I go college in September.

Michael   Is it?

Lou   Yep.

Michael   Ah, that's heavy.

Lou   I know.

Michael   Nice. So what you gonna study?

Lou   Well, I was thinking fashion design. And beauty therapy and styling was always in the mix . . .

Michael   Yeah, you've always had that on lock. Just the right person.

Lou   Yeah, but everything seems to be going towards being a make-up artist. I mean that's everything / in one.

Bernice   Sorry, so why you here?

Lou   Pardon?

Michael   Bernice, man.

Bernice   No hold on, why is she here?

Lou   You don't need to know. I come to speak to your brother.

Bernice   Yeah, but you come knocking at my door.

Lou   Yes, but I didn't come for you.

Michael   Bee, could you just let us talk?

Bernice   No, Michael. I don't trust this gel.

Lou   Here we go.

Bernice   I never trusted you.

Lou   Why? What have I done to you?

Bernice   You ask that with your reputation?

Lou   No. What have I ever done to you?

Bernice   Oh whatever.

Lou   Nah, it's not whatever. Come on, what have I / done to you?

Michael   Come just leave it.

Bernice   Thank you.

Michael   Nah, both of you. Please.

Couple beats.

Bernice   And what about her parasite brother, makin' up noise, stinking up mum's living room, coming eating our food.

Lou   Nah nah nah hold on.

Bernice   Distracting my brother . . .

Michael   No he ain't.

Bernice   Yes he is.

Michael   He doesn't.

Bernice   And he's / a fucking weirdo.

Lou   / Don't talk about my brother like that.

Bernice   I'm just stating the facts, can't argue with that.

Lou   'Stating the facts'. Go fuck yourself.

Michael   Nah 'old on, man, 'old on.

Lou   Talkin' like he's nuffin'. Like you even know him. Who are *you*? Who are *you*?

Bernice   Well, I ain't never been where you just been, that's for sure.

Lou   Oh, ok ok.

Bernice   Probably be back there in a couple weeks.

Lou   So that's how it is, yeah?

Bernice   Yeah.

Lou   That's how you wanna play it?

Both on their feet and facing each other by now.

Bernice   Yeah.

Lou   You wanna take it there?

Bernice   Yeah.

Lou   Dass where you wanna take it?

Bernice   Yeah and I'll fucking rip you apart.

Lou   You try it you try it.

Bernice   I will. Trust me I will.

Lou   Come on then, let's go.

Michael   No! You ain't gonna do that. You ain't doing that.

Bernice   Yeah, just dash her out!

Michael   Bernice, can you please just leave us.

Bernice   No, Michael. I ain't movin'. This is my house.

Michael   Please! Come, man.

Bernice   No.

Michael   Let me sort this. Please?

Bernice   Oh, whatever. I seriously ain't got time for this gel, anyway.

She ain't nuttin' but a raass.

Turns and walks off.

Lou   Wow, she is good.

Michael   Look, Lou, what you want?

Lou   You know what I want.

Michael   Nah, man. I can't.

Lou   Michael.

Michael   I can't.

Lou   I got a right.

Michael   I know but / he don't want

Lou   / Where is he?

Michael   He don't want me to tell no one.

Lou   I'm his sister.

Michael   I promised him.

Lou   Why? What's the big secret?

Michael   I don't know . . . I just know . . .

Lou   What?

Michael   He don't want to see you.

Lou   They've put him in a hostel, haven't they? I knew it! Michael, he will not survive there.

Michael   Look, he don't want to talk to you, that's all. I'm sorry.

Lou *gets out a cigarette and lights up.*

Lou   So what's he doing?

Michael   Bwoy, college.

Lou   College?

Michael   Well he did enrol.

Lou   Yeah that's my Gary.

Michael   Yeah.

Lou   That's why he needs me. Do you understand?

Michael   Yeah.

Lou *hands cigarette to* **Michael**.

Michael   Safe.

He smokes.

Lou   I am getting that flat.

Michael   Yeah?

Lou   Yeah, been down Housing. They said two months, maybe three and I'll have a place. I'm getting everything sorted.

Michael   Yeah.

Lou   This time, Michael, I can do it. I'm gonna do it.

Michael   Yeah yeah.

Lou   I will.

Michael   For sure.

Lou   I'm in a good place now. Eight months, Michael. (*Rolls up sleeve.*) See?

Michael   What?

Lou   Nothing.

Michael   Oh . . . oh right. Wow!

Lou   Vitamins. Gym. Whole new start. That's why I know I can do it, ya know?

Michael   Yeah, I do.

Lou   I'm going to be totally there for him. It'll be just me and Gary. Where is he? Which hostel? Come on, Michael.

Michael   I can't.

Lou   He needs me. You know him, he needs looking after.

Michael   He's cool.

Lou   You don't understand. Once they push you out you're in freefall, you're on your fucking own.

Michael   I don't know . . .

Lou   What?

Michael   If it can happen, Lou. I'm sorry.

Lou   No, that's what I'm saying, I am going to make it happen.

Michael *smokes. She watches him.*

Lou   What about you? You must be at uni now, ennit?

Michael   Nah, next year. I still gotta finish exams.

Lou   Is it going alright?

Michael   Yeah, it's alright.

Lou   You'll get straight A's, anyway.

Michael   Boy, we'll see.

Lou   'Course you will. I know you. You're gonna do well.

Michael   We'll see . . . Yeah . . .

Lou   So what you gonna do?

Michael   What?

Lou   At university.

Michael   Psychology.

Lou   Ah, all about people's minds. So can you tell what I'm thinking now?

Michael *laughs.*

Lou   Well? Can you?

Michael   'Course not.

Lou   No?

Michael   No.

Lou   Sure?

Michael   No. I mean, yeah.

Lou *is looking at* **Michael**.

Michael   What?

Lou   What?

Michael   What you looking at?

Lou   I'm looking at you.

Michael   Yeah . . . It's good to see you.

Lou   Yeah. It is.

She strokes his cheek, kisses where she's stroked and moves in closer. He puts his arms around her and she begins to kiss his lips.

Lights fade.

Scene Seven

Michael *and* **Bernice**'s *living room.* **Fog**, **Lou** *and* **Michael** *are there.*

Fog   Nah, I'm gone. I'm gone.

Goes to leave but **Lou** *blocks his way.*

Lou   Gary.

Fog   Move from me.

Lou   Why you never / pick up?

Fog   Shut up.

Lou Why you never / text me back?

Fog Move!

Lou Nah, listen to me!

Fog Come out my way.

Lou No.

Fog Who's dis gel? Who's dis / gel?

Lou I just wanna talk to you.

Fog Nah, you're nuts. Come out my way. (*To* **Michael**.)
What da fuck, man! What da fuck? Why she here? Why you
bring her here?

Michael Maybe let her talk, bruv.

Fog Nah, she ain't sayin' nuttin'. Get her out.

Michael Bruv?

Fog Get her out!

Lou Just talk to me.

Fog I got shit to do. Money to make. Ain't got time for
dis bitch.

Lou *gives him a look that's familiar to him.*

Fog What?

Lou What?

Fog Don't do that.

Lou What?

Fog Don't fucking do that!

Lou So you don't need me now?

Fog What? Me need you? Shuttup, I never did I never did.

Lou So you alright?

Fog Yeah 'course.

Lou   Yeah?

Fog   Yeah I'm cool.

Lou   Yeah?

Fog   Yes!

Lou   So everything cool yeah. Brock House alright yeah?

No response.

Lou   You likin' it dere, yeah?

Fog   Yeah. Yeah's good now you're gone. Man's top now, ennit.

Lou   Seen . . . So how's all your boys? How's de man dem?

Fog   Yeah.

Lou   How's Jason and that?

Fog   Yeah, dere fuckin' good, man, dere good.

Lou   Why you lying? Why you fuckin' lying to me? You ain't there no more.

Fog   Yes I am!

Lou   Michael told me. You're with Dad.

Fog   Why did you say that? Why you telling her?

Michael   I just . . .

Fog   You're a dickhead. You're a dickhead!

Lou   We *swore* . . . didn't we?

No response.

Lou   Didn't we, Gary?

Fog   I don't remember.

Lou   Yes, you do. 'Course you do! We swore we'd never talk to him. We hate him!

Fog   No I don't.

Lou   Yes you do. And you know why.

Fog   No I don't.

Lou   You forgotten what he did to Mum?

Fog   No. Yeah. No nothing.

Lou   We swore and you can't go back on that. You can't!

Fog   I ain't.

Lou   You have.

Fog   I ain't!

Lou   Yes you have!

Fog   He's safe now. Got me television. Plasma / wide screen.

Lou   You broke your promise for a fuckin' television!

Fog   Fuckin' bought it, TV, for me.

Lou   So what? What about me?

Fog   Shuttup.

Lou   You weren't even gonna tell me.

Fog   Nah nah, fuck this.

Lou   Were you? Were you? (*Couple beats.*) Does he ask about me?

Fog   No.

Lou   He ain't said nothing?

Fog   Yeah.

Lou   What?

Fog   He said he hates you. You fucked him up, with that letter. That I didn't want you to send! He don't never wanna see you again.

Beat.

Lou   So what, it's you and him now, yeah? (*Pushes him.*) You and him. Happy little twosome. (*Pushes him really hard.*) Yeah?

Michael   Hey, calm it, man.

Lou   Yeah, nice, nice. Ain't dat nice? Nice TV.

Michael   Oi, hold it down, Lou.

He restrains her.

Fog   I'm gonna knock this bitch out.

Lou   What have I got?

Fog   Shut up!

Michael   Just stop it, man.

Lou   What 'ave I got?

Fog   Shut up shut up, it's your fault.

Lou   My fault?

Fog   Yeah, little fuckin' slag!

Lou   What?

Fog   Fuckin' whore.

Michael   Bruv, shut up. What you playing at?

Fog   Shut up.

Michael   No, you can't speak to her like that.

Fog   Shut up!

Michael   She's your sister.

Fog   She ain't nothing.

Lou *looks him dead in the eyes.*

Fog   What? What da fuck she lookin' at? Little slag. Look at her, little slag. What? Don't fuckin' look at me. I'll knock you out lookin' at me.

Yeah go on, go on, bruv, have a go.

Michael   Shut the fuck up.

Fog   Nah, go on, have a piece of this bitch. Everyone else has.

Lou   Are you that dumb?

Fog   Nah, you're dumb, you're dumb.

Lou   You know why that happened. Don't you?

Fog   I don't give a fuck.

Lou   'Cos you wouldn't stick up for yourself.

Fog   Bare shit bare shit talk!

Lou   Locked you naked in the cupboard broke your arm.

Fog   I'm gonna kill you!

Lou   And you just come out smiling like a little idiot.

Michael   Stop it! Fucking both of you stop it!

Just listen to yourselves, man.

Couple beats.

Lou   Look, I got a flat. Just for us. Like we said.

Fog   I don't want it.

Lou   Come on.

Fog   Don't wanna live with a slag.

He goes to leave, she stops him.

Lou   Gary

Fog   I'm Fog man, Fog get the fuck!

Lou   I get it I get it. It's all new, yeah? Dad comes back. Getting you nice things. All nice. Then I come back. And it gets confusing. 'Cos the plans you and me made don't seem so good now. 'Course you're gonna feel like that. At first. But what about when he goes? Leaves you again? 'Cos he will. You know he will. What you gonna do? What will you have? Where you gonna go? Gary?

Fog   You done now?

He goes.

Lou   Gary. Gary please come back!

Scene Eight

Cannon *and* **Fog**'s *flat in the dark. TV screen is a white fuzz, providing the only light.* **Fog** *enters lounge and goes to the window /audience. The song he sings in this scene is 'Original Nuttah' by Apache Indian and Shy FX.*

Fog   What, are you mad? Are you mad? You mad? What, are you mad? Fuckin' dickhead. I'll bang you in your head! Put my ring in your face, rude boy!

He paces round the room.

Oi fuck off G fuck off G F-O-G what G F-O-G fuck off G.

He catches himself reflected in the balcony window. He smiles.

What you smilin' for? Who you smilin' at? Why you smilin'? Gone out smilin' like a little idiot.

You pussy 'ole! Are you nuts? Are you nuts, blud? What? What what what?!

(*Very suddenly he sing-shouts*) 'I am a murderer . . .'

A long moment of absolute stillness and silence as he studies his reflection. Very suddenly he kicks a chair. It topples over, weighted by **Cannon**'s *leather jacket. He puts on jacket. He pulls imaginary gun out of inside pocket. Unseen by* **Fog**, **Cannon** *appears in the doorway. He stands and watches.*

Fog   Get on da floor. I said get on da floor. On da floor! Now! Get your money out. How much ya got? Pass dat. Pass dat. Gimme dat chain!

He laughs and walks around room in silence, strong, controlled and sustained. Stops suddenly, opens jacket and inhales **Cannon**'s *scent for a long moment.*

Fog (*starts singing*)   'Ye never know de gangsta
  Me say live inna jungle. Whey-eyheyeah.'

He continues singing the song, moving his body to the rhythm, while building in intensity. He becomes increasingly manic, jumping and throwing his body around the room.

  'I am a nuttah
  Original man-ma-man-ma-man nuttah
  Original manamanamanamanamanamana . . .'

He keeps on going until suddenly he realises **Cannon**'s *presence. They look at each other.* **Cannon** *leaves.*

Scene Nine

Cannon *and* **Fog**'s *flat.* Dragon Ball Z *on TV. A couple of dead beers on the floor.* **Cannon** *stands in vest and old tracksuit bottom. He faces* **Lou**.

Cannon   I didn't realise . . . You look so like . . . So . . . So you're here? So you're not . . . 'Cos I've been looking for you. Everywhere . . .Where you been?

No response.

Cannon   You've grown. You've grown up. 'Course you have. Well, don't stand on ceremony, sit yourself down then.

She doesn't.

Cannon   Yeah, we're alright. It's alright here. It's good. Small. But not that small. Four rooms not counting . . . Yeah, plenty of room plenty. It'll do. For the time being anyway. God you're the image of her. I was just about to paint.

Pause.

Where's my fags?

He goes through his pockets and gets out cigarettes.

He's nicked my lighter again. That boy.

So . . . yeah . . . so . . . it's good, yeah . . . great . . . you're here. Here we are . . .

Hello. It's good to see you.

No response.

Gary said you'd gone away? Where ya been? Somewhere nice?

No response.

Cannon   Something wrong? Louise?

No response.

Cannon   It was only meant to be a one-off. I know I know . . . that must sound bad enough but . . . I never meant it to go on, it's just . . . your mum had been so . . . tired, 'course I didn't know why at the time or I never would of . . . Never. Honest to God . . . You don't know what it's like, Louise, it . . . it had just been hard. Hard time for both of us. Do you understand, love?

Lou   I sucked their dicks every night.

Cannon   Wh't?

Lou   At Brock House. Jason, Simeon. Patrick. Simeon used to like to fuck my mouth. Like it was a cunt. Make me choke.

Cannon   Don't be disgusting.

Lou   I let them.

Cannon   Why you telling me this?

Lou   I let them.

Cannon   I'm not listening.

Lou   Whatever they wanted.

Cannon   No!

Lou   Sometimes they'd line up / and do it.

Cannon   No no no you're just trying to upset me.

Lou   No, I'm not.

Cannon   You're being foul-mouthed and nasty just / to upset me.

Lou   / Why don't you believe me?

Cannon   It's ridiculous.

Lou   It's true.

Cannon   Louise, you're a lovely girl. Beautiful. It's horrible to hear all that stuff coming out your mouth.

Lou   You weren't there.

Cannon   I know. I know. I wasn't . . . for a while. For a long while . . . But I'm here now, that's what's important. Hey, my love . . .

He moves closer to her.

Come here. It's alright. It's gonna be alright. I'm here now. I'm here for my little girl.

Lou   You left your little girl . . .

Cannon   Shhh . . . shhh . . . shhh . . . and I'm sorry . . .

Lou   Now she don't exist.

Lights out.

Scene Ten

Cannon *and* **Fog**'*s flat. The two armchairs are now side by side. There are empty beer bottles and cans, takeaway pizza boxes and their remains on trestle and floor.* **Cannon** *and* **Fog**, *in T-shirts, sit together watching an Amir Khan fight on TV. The commentary can be heard under their voices.*

Cannon   See? Discipline. Discipline and control. Watch him. I want you to watch him closely. See? That's how you get your focus.

Fog   Yeah, man, focus. Focus.

Cannon   Watch him move. Beautiful. Dances, see? Dances like Ali. Floats like a butterfly . . . Hook him, you cunt!

Fog   Yeah man!

Cannon   Come on! . . . Come on. Right jab! And again! Right right! . . .

Fog (*slightly cockney*)   Jab 'im! Jab 'im! Come on, Khan!

Sudden silence, both nod their heads ten times.

Both   Out!

Cannon   Yes!

Fog (*like an echo*)   Yes!

Cannon   See that?

Fog   Yes.

Cannon   Did ja see that?

Fog   I saw it! I saw it!

Cannon   You saw that, didn't ya? Right cross, left uppercut.

They both do it, still seated, facing TV.

Cannon   Cross, uppercut, cross uppercut, right left, right left. Beautiful combination. You gotta learn that one. Look, look. Check the replay.

Fog   Yeah yeah.

Cannon   Right to the head. See that? Power. Then look, look, drops his shoulder – very important – and *up* with the left.

Fog   Yes!

They repeat the combination again several times.

Cannon   Right left.

Fog   Right left.

Cannon   Mate, 97, that year, I tell you . . . June . . . June 1997 . . . that was a fight! Ah, mate, you should've been there . . .

Fog   Yeah.

Cannon   That was *the* fight, I'm telling you . . . that was . . . I wish you could've seen me.

Fog   Yeah!

Cannon   Yeah, you should've seen me . . . No . . . wait . . . wait! Hold on, wait there, don't move. Don't move!

He jumps up and leaves room excitedly. **Fog** *sits up straight in chair, not moving.* **Cannon** *returns holding a belt with a silver buckle.*

Cannon   'Ere, look at this.

Fog   I didn't move.

Cannon   Ey?

Fog   I didn't move.

Cannon   Oh. Look. Look at this – Inter-regimental Light Heavyweight Champion.

Fog   Shit, man. That's deep.

Cannon   Ey? Ey? Woja fink? Woja fink? (*Trying to squeeze waist into belt.*) It's shrunk, mate.

Fog   Is it?

Cannon   That's no good. Gotta get rid of some of this. Get down the gym, shed some pounds.

Fog   Get into shape.

Cannon   Yep. Get fit get fit get fit. Hup hup hup hup.

Cannon *does a high-step jog out of the room.* **Fog** *picks up belt, holds it a moment and slowly puts it on.* **Cannon** *re-enters with two pairs of boxing gloves.*

Cannon   Oh? Yeah. Yeah, it fits you.

Fog   Yeah?

Cannon   Look at these. Know what these are? Ey? Know what these are? They're history. Family history. I shed blood with these.

Fog   Shit, man!

Cannon   Yeah, they'll tell you. They got the story writ on them in blood. See?

Fog   Yeah.

Cannon   Yeah. Men still remember that fight. Me, I lived every second of it.

He hands the other pair to **Fog** *and puts on 'bloodied' pair.*

Cannon   OK. So we go five rounds punch for punch. Not a point separating us. That close. One of us gotta finish it.

Fog *puts on other pair of gloves.*

Cannon   Come the sixth we're both on our feet before the bell. This is the kill. Smell of blood, in the ring, in the crowd. Crowd like an animal roaring for it. In the ring, just me and him. No before. No after. Only now.

Both strip off their T-shirts. On TV bell sounds.

Cannon   Seconds out, round six.

They face each other.

Cannon   He's southpaw. Southpaw.

Fog *changes stance to lead with his right hand.*

Cannon   OK, he's in fast. Throws everything at me. Come on come on!

Bang! Gotcha! And again. And again.

Cannon, *wanting to re-enact his fight, calls directions to* **Fog** *who attempts to follow them. As this continues,* **Cannon** *becomes more* *frustrated and more sergeant-majorly.* **Fog** *is increasingly bewildered and unable.*

Cannon   Left hook. Left! To my chin, like I showed ya. Chin, here, under me nose! Left, I said. Left! That's it. Come on . . . go on, get your feet moving. Right cross. Right cross. Come on concentrate.

Fog   I am.

Cannon   It's like fighting with a girl. Come on! Come on, what's the matter with ya? Go on, get your guard up! Get your bloody guard up, man!

Fog's *arms go up and* **Cannon** *punches him twice lightly in the stomach.*

Cannon   What you doin'? Left yourself wide open.

Fog's *arms go down to protect his stomach and* **Cannon** *jabs him on the chin.*

Cannon   Doiyng! Guard guard. Where's your guard?

He drops his own arms, dances around **Fog**, *giving him jabs where he's unprotected.*

Doiyng! Doiyng!

Fog *stops.*

Cannon   What's the matter wiv ya? Why you fucking about? Come on get a move on, get a bloody move on!

Suddenly **Fog** *lunges at him with a battery of flailing punches.* **Cannon** *doesn't punch back, but is forced to block and back away. When both are out of breath, they lean in on each other,* **Fog** *making a few weak kidney punches, before he's still. They remain in this position for a few moments.* **Cannon** *drops his arms.* **Fog** *opens his fists and begins to hug his father closer and closer. He nestles his face and his open lips into* **Cannon**'s *neck.* **Cannon** *stands still for a moment.*

Cannon   What you doin'? What you doin'?

Fog *is unable to stop himself.*

Cannon   What the fuck you doin'!

He violently pushes **Fog** *to the floor.*

Cannon   What you doin'?

Fog *curls up in a ball.* **Cannon** *bends over him and shouts/roars at his head.*

Cannon   Arrrgggghhhh you useless piece of shit!

He walks out of the room. Lights down on **Fog**. *TV remains on and commentary continues.*

Scene Eleven

In **Michael** *and* **Bernice**'s *living room, same as before, except for the presence of an ironing board and iron. TV is on MTV Base.* **Michael** *coming in followed by* **Fog**. **Fog** *sits and* **Michael** *hovers near the ironing board.*

Fog   Who's here?

Michael   What?

Fog   Who's here?

Michael   My sister. She's getting ready.

Fog   For what?

Michael   The interview.

Fog   Seen.

He gets out his spliff gear and starts to roll.

Michael   Hold it down, bruv.

Fog   What?

Michael   Just wait till she's gone.

Fog *continues to roll.*

Michael   Oy . . . oy.

Fog   I'm just billing, man. Ain't gonna smoke da t'ing. Man needs to relax a bit, ya get me. Stop workin' yourself up.

Michael   Yeah yeah cool, man.

Fog   Yeah, cool. Sit down, ennit.

Michael   In a bit . . . Look, bruv, this thing . . . I didn't wanna get involved, I didn't even know she was back in the manor.

Fog   Man needs to bell up Simeon, get some more of this high grade. It's selling quick.

Michael   I saw her in Chick King and she begged me, you know like crying and shit, said she needed to see you and I didn't know / what to do.

Fog   Shut up! (*Beat.*) I forgive you, alright. Done. Dusted. In the past.

Bernice   Michael? (*Rushes in.*) Michael!

Michael   Oh yeah yeah, sorry, Bea.

Bernice   Come on then.

Michael   I'm doing it.

He irons her top.

Fog   Joke t'ing.

Bernice (*holds up earrings*)   So what, these ones or these?

Michael   Uhm . . .

Bernice   Come on, Michael. These, or these?

Michael   Yeah.

Bernice   Which?

Michael   The blue ones.

Bernice   OK cool. You nearly finished?

Michael   Yeah, one minute.

Bernice   Hurry up.

Exits.

Michael   Boy she takes the piss, man.

Fog   Don't 'ave it den.

Michael   Wha'?

Fog   Don't have it from her. Don't let her take da piss like dat. Always talkin' down to you and shit. You're too weak, blud. Too weak. Weak. Ya know what I'm sayin', blud?

Michael   Yeah.

Fog   Y'know what I'm sayin'?

Michael   Yes!

Fog   Fuck it, man. It's all good anyway . . . you safe? You safe? . . . Yeah. Yeah, we're gonna shock it out dis weekend. Stratford Rex, blud. I can't wait. I can't wait! Gonna rave it out at Rex. Pop a champs. Blaze a zoot wi' my boy. I can't wait.

Michael   I can't come.

Fog   Are you jokin'?

Michael   Nah, bruv, I'm lookin' at dat uni.

Fog   What? 11 oclock at night when da raves on?

Michael   Yeah, I won't make it back.

Fog   What?

Michael   That night. It's too far.

Fog   What, you goin' like . . . 'undred miles or suttin'?

Michael   I think it's about two hundred. Gotta stay da night.

Fog   Stay for what?

Michael Just to look round. See if I / like it.

Fog So you're not comin' rave.

Michael Can't.

Fog You're gonna be dere?

Michael Yeah. 'Cause if I like it I might make it my / first choice.

Fog OK. OK, so you not coming den, yeah? Yeah?

Michael Yeah,

Fog That's alright. That's alright. It's all good . . . rave it out. On my jacks. On my jacks.

He goes back to billing up. There is a grime video playing on TV. **Michael** *watches.*

Fog Oy, what the fuck you watchin', blud?

Michael What?

Fog Don't watch dem, dey look like pop stars now. Pop stars, rude boy.

Michael Yeah.

Fog Try leave road.

Michael Yeah, cool, man.

Fog Dey ain't cool. Dey ain't real. Come out da manor an' dey fink dere big. Try leave da man dem behind, y'kna. Try leave us behind. You know what, man should stamp on dem. Stamp on dem batty boy. (*To TV.*) Yeah, we know where you live now – Hertfordshire – hundred miles and shit – seen you on MTV Cribs. Hertfordshire! I'm gonna come down your ends, boy – tax your whip, boy.

Bernice *enters, takes top.*

Bernice Perfect. (*Holds it against herself.*) Or does it look too young?

Michael   No.

Bernice   OK. You sure?

Michael   Yes, man. Hurry up.

Bernice   Gimme another question.

Michael (*picks up list*)   OK – 'This company has an equal opportunities policy – what do you understand by that?'

Bernice   That no one should be discriminated against on the grounds of race, religion, age, gender, sexuality etcetera etcetera etcetera and everyone should be included in everything all of the time. Good. Done. Right, let's go. (*She rushes out, calling.*) Thanks, Michael.

Michael *slowly winds iron lead.* **Fog** *smiles to himself.*

Fog   Yeah, man saw Chantelle today. Boy! Firm arse, y' get me? Some nice firmness.

Michael   Yeah, her arse is bangin'.

Fog   Yes!

Michael   Yeah.

Fog   Oi, I should speech dat, blud.

Michael   Yeah.

Fog   Get some nice sex out of dat one. I should pounce on dat, blud. Tap dat, fuck dat blaze dat smack dat! Finish dat, so she don't fuckin' forget.

Silence. **Fog** *is billing up spliff.*

Fog   Two hundred . . .

Michael   Uh?

Fog   Two hundred miles.

Michael   Yeah, I know. Proper mission. Proper mission. (*Beat.*) Man'll have to stay up there, y'know. Whole term. Just come back for Christmas and shit.

Fog   I need to get my car. Need to get it quick.
  Pull up in my whip
  Beep beep, BM, Audi TT
  Blacked out windows
  So I can see you
  But ya can't / see me.

Michael   Yeah man, it's gonna be hard up there. Bare studying.

Fog   Yeah, bare boffin shit. But it's your t'ing, your t'ing, I know.

Michael   And I'm gonna have to get a job as well up there, pay off my student loan.

Fog   Nah, fuck dat shit, you can work for me. I'll set you up. Couple ounces.

Some whites. Keep it all ticking over when I'm not dere.

Michael   Nah, don't be stupid, man. I can't do that shit.

Fog   Why not?

Michael   If I get caught I'm getting kicked out.

Fog   Pussy hole.

Michael   Nah, just shut the fuck up! Just listen for / once.

Bernice (*entering*)   So what d'ya think? If you don't like it, I'm not changing. Do you like it?

Michael   Yeah man, you look good.

Bernice   Yeah?

Michael   Definite.

Bernice   Good. Last question. The one about . . .

Michael   Yeah yeah. (*Reads.*) 'Who do you think . . . Why do you think you are the right candidate for this post?'

Bernice   'Cos ya said so. No, serious, Bernice. Because I have been with Langley and Masons ever since I left school, so I have a detailed knowledge of the company's 'mission', aims, policies and procedures. (*Takes a breath.*) And I'm fantastic.

Michael   Fine. You're ready, Bea.

Bernice   OK. Wish me luck.

Michael   Good luck, but you don't need it.

Bernice   OK, bye.

She turns to go.

Fog   Good luck.

Bernice (*turning back*)   Oh? Thanks . . . Thank you. See ya later.

She exits.

Fog *gets a knife out of his pocket and lays it on the table between them. He lights his spliff, has a few tokes, then offers to* **Michael**.

Michael   Nah.

Fog   Go on.

Michael   No.

Fog   Come blud, need to relax a bit.

Michael   I don't.

Fog   What's wrong with you?

Michael   Nothing!

Fog   Come, just have some.

He holds out spliff right in front of him. **Michael** *brushes* **Fog**'s *arm away.*

Michael   Come off me, man.

Fog   You're weird, blud. You know you're getting weird.

Beat. **Fog** *gets out his phone.*

Yeah, man needs to make a couple calls. Business is growing. I need some protection, need to get tooled up. Start carrying a piece.

Michael   Stop it, man.

Fog   Nah. Can't be getting jacked on road. Man try take my shit, man get shot. Simple. I don't care. I don't care. Dis is a serious t'ing. Man needs to know. And if them posh boys at your uni fink they can take man for an idiot, man'll show them the way.

Michael   No you won't.

Fog   Nah nah nah, so they know not to fuck with me and my boy. Ya get me?

Michael   What you talkin' 'bout, stop talking like that.

Fog   No, you, you stop it.

Michael   Talkin' shit. Always talkin' shit. What you even gonna do?

Fog   What? What?

Michael   What you gonna do? Who you gonna bring?

Fog   What! (*He grabs the knife.*) I'll come down there, bruv, take you all out.

Michael   No you won't. You ain't gonna do nothing.

Fog   I'll do what I want.

Michael   No you won't.

Fog   I will.

They look at each other over a great distance.

Michael   You can't come.

Fog   Who says?

Michael   Me. I don't want you there.

Fog   Yes you do.

Michael   No I don't. They'll laugh at you. They'll laugh at me.

Couple beats.

Michael   Look all I'm sayin' bruv is . . . it's gonna be mad. Ya know? They're mad places these unis. Mad characters. World of their own . . . totally different.

You wouldn't like it. And . . . and it's gonna be busy. Lot of work at uni. Mad lot of work . . . you know? But it's cool 'cos the great thing is I'll get long holidays. Then I'll come back down and see all the man dem.

Fog   Don't worry, blud.

Michael   What?

Fog   It's cool.

Michael   Yeah?

Fog   Yeah, man.

Michael   OK. Yeah, and we'll do our shit in the holidays.

Fog *gathers all his spliff-making stuff up and gets up.*

Michael   Yeah, I'll be ready for it by then. Get my head out of all dem books. I'll be proper ready, ready to chill.

Fog   Nah, man.

Michael   Ey?

Fog   Stay with your books, blud.

Michael   What?

Fog   'Cos you won't be welcome here. Man leaves he don't come back. He don't come back.

He leaves.

Scene Twelve

Early next morning. Lights up on **Cannon** *and* **Fog**'s *front room.*
Socks, boxers and a jumper are drying over armchairs and the
tricycle. **Cannon** *enters with a holdall, which he puts down. He*
gathers up each article of washing, folds it neatly and quickly packs
it in the holdall. He takes an empty, used envelope from his pocket
and, resting on top of the TV, scribbles a note. He takes out his wallet
and extracts fifteen £20 notes, which he puts in the envelope. He
puts his wallet back in his pocket and puts the envelope on the tricycle
seat. He hesitates, gets out wallet and begins to put five more £20 in
the envelope, when he hears the front door open. He quickly stuffs
the envelope into his jacket pocket and tries to hide the holdall behind
him. After some moments **Fog** *enters.*

Cannon   Hello, mate. You was out all night, then. Have a
good one? Good night out?

Fog   Yeah.

Cannon   Sweet sweet.

Fog   Yeah.

Cannon   What, bin out on the town? Dancin' and alla that?

Fog   Yeah yeah,

Cannon   Ah, fantastic. That's good to hear. Just what you
should be doin' at your age. (*Beat.*) Any ladies?

Fog   Yeah.

Cannon   Yeah?

Fog   Yeah, dere was a few.

Cannon   Ah, lovely jubbly.

Fog   I didn't know what one to pick.

Cannon   One with the biggest tits I'd say. Ey?

Fog   Yeah . . .

Cannon   So which one?

Fog What?

Cannon Which one did you pick?

Fog Uh, the one with the biggest tits.

Cannon Nice one.

Fog Yeah . . . she was proper on me all night.

Cannon Ah, good man. Good man.

Beat.

Fog / She wouldn't leave me alone.

Cannon / So what's her name? What?

Fog Uh?

Cannon So it was a good one, yeah?

Fog Yeah . . . it was heavy.

Cannon Nice. So she was a bit of alright, then? Bit of alright?

Fog Yeah, she was fit.

Cannon (*beat*) Good music?

Fog Yeah, it was alright. MCs were alright.

Cannon Right. Nah, that's good. I'm so glad you had a good time.

Fog Yeah, I did . . . I had a good time.

Cannon Yeah, a good time was had by all. That's what it's all about, ennit? Can't get better than that. Ain't that true?

Fog For real.

Cannon I mean, do it while you're young. Do it while you can. You're only young once, ya know. Gotta enjoy yourself, ain't ya?

Fog Yeah.

Cannon   Yeah, you go for it while you can. Only one chance, you hear me?

That's all you get.

He grips **Fog**'s *upper arms and looks intently into his eyes.*

Gotta take it. Gotta take it.

Searches in pockets.

I'm out of fags. I'll just pop out.

He goes towards the door.

Fog   Dad.

Cannon *stops and turns towards* **Fog**.

Fog   You forgot your bag.

They look at each other a long moment.

Blackout.

Authors' Postscript

There are over 59,000 children in care in the UK at any one time.[1]

45% of children in care are assessed as having a mental health disorder, compared to 10% of children in the general population.[2]

30% of children in custody have been in the care system.

Whilst care leavers represent 1% of the UK population, they make up 23% of the prison population.

42% of young women prostitutes interviewed in a 2006 research paper had been in care at some point in their lives.

Parents who have themselves been in care are twice as likely to lose the right to keep their own children.

Theoretically, there is after-care, but it can be very patchy. Very often it is as Lou says:

'Once they push you out you're in freefall, you're on your fucking own.'

[1] The Fostering Network, www.fostering.net

[2] These and all subsequent statistics from: Gentleman, Amelia, 'Children in Care: how Britain is failing its most vulnerable', *The Guardian*, 20 April 2009 <http://www.guardian.co.uk/society/2009/apr/20/care-system-failures>